ProMgmt.®

Food and Beverage Cost Control

SECOND EDITION

National Restaurant Association
EDUCATIONAL FOUNDATION
175 W. Jackson Boulevard, Suite 1500, Chicago, IL 60604
To reorder call 800-765-2122 (312-715-1010 in Chicagoland)
www.nraef.org

t Workbook

National Restaurant Association
EDUCATIONAL FOUNDATION

JOHN WILEY & SONS, INC.

ProMgmt. is a registered trademark of the National Restaurant Association Educational Foundation.

This student workbook is designed to be used with the textbook *Food and Beverage Cost Control, Second Edition* by Jack E. Miller, David K. Hayes, and Lea R. Dopson.

This book is printed on acid-free paper. ∞

Published by John Wiley & Sons, Inc., New York.

Published simultaneously in Canada.

This publication is designed to provide accurate and authoritative information in regard to the subject matter covered. It is sold with the understanding that the publisher is not engaged in rendering professional services. If professional advice or other expert assistance is required, the services of a competent professional person should be sought.

Library of Congress Cataloging-in-Publication Data:

ISBN: 0-471-14993-4

Printed in the United States of America.

10 9 8 7 6 5 4 3

Contents

Introduction

Food and Beverage Cost Control, Second Edition is designed to introduce future foodservice managers to the importance of cost control throughout the operation. Cost control management is necessary in order for the operation to maximize profits and operate successfully. Students will learn the basics concerning food, beverage, and labor cost controls, and also learn to apply basic accounting principles to cost control.

The course begins with a discussion of how to manage income and expenses and determine sales volume. It then examines managing the costs of food, beverages, labor, and the food and beverage production process. Controlling other expenses and analyzing results using basic accounting are covered next. The course concludes with a discussion of maintaining security and improving income controls through computer use.

How to Earn a ProMgmt℠ Certificate of Course Completion

To earn a ProMgmt. Certificate of Course Completion, a student must complete all student workbook exercises and receive a passing score on the final examination.

To apply for the ProMgmt. Certificate of Course Completion, complete the registration portion of the examination answer sheet on the inside front cover of this workbook and give it to your instructor, who will then forward it to the National Restaurant Association Educational Foundation.

Each student registered with the Educational Foundation will receive a student number. Please make a record of it; this number will identify you during your present and future coursework with the Educational Foundation.

ProMgmt. certificate requirements are administered exclusively through colleges and other educational institutions that offer ProMgmt. courses and examinations.

If you are not currently enrolled in a ProMgmt. course and would like to earn a ProMgmt. certificate, please contact your local educational institution to see if they are willing to administer the ProMgmt. certificate requirements for non-enrolled students. You can also visit **www.edfound.org** for a list of ProMgmt. Partner schools. ProMgmt. Partner schools offer seven or more courses that include administration of the ProMgmt. certificate requirements.

The Educational Foundation leaves it to the discretion of each educational institution offering ProMgmt. courses to decide whether or not that institution will administer the ProMgmt. certificate requirements to non-enrolled students. If an institution does administer ProMgmt. certificate requirements to non-enrolled students, that institution may charge an additional fee, of an amount determined by that institution, for the administration of the ProMgmt. certificate requirements.

Course Materials

This course consists of the text, *Food and Beverage Cost Control, Second Edition* by Jack E. Miller, David K. Hayes, and Lea Dopson, the student workbook, and a final examination. The examination is the final section of your course and is sent to an instructor for administration, then returned to the Educational Foundation for grading.

Each lesson consists of:
- Student objectives
- Reading assignment
- Chapter exercises

At the end of the Workbook you will find:
- A study outline of the textbook
- A glossary (when the textbook does not have one)
- An 80-question practice test
- Answers to the practice test

The objectives indicate what you can expect to learn from the course, and are designed to help you organize your studying and concentrate on important topics and explanations. Refer to the objectives frequently to make sure you are meeting them.

The exercises help you check how well you've learned the concepts in each chapter. These will be graded by your instructor.

An 80-question practice test appears at the end of the workbook. All the questions are multiple-choice and have four possible answers. Circle the best answer to each question, as in this example:

Who was the first president of the United States?
  A. Thomas Jefferson
  B. George Washington
  C. Benjamin Franklin
  D. John Adams

Answers to the practice test follow in the workbook so that you may grade your own work.

The Final Exam

All examinations may first be graded by your instructor and then officially graded again by the Educational Foundation. If you do not receive a passing grade on the examination, you may request a retest. A retest fee will be charged for the second examination.

Study Tips

Since you have already demonstrated an interest in furthering your foodservice education by registering for this Educational Foundation course, you know that your next step is study preparation. We have included some specific study pointers which you may find useful.

- Build studying into your routine. If you hold a full-time job, you need to take a realistic approach to studying. Set aside a specific time and place to study, and stick to your routine as closely as possible. Your study area should have room for your course materials and any other necessary study aids. If possible, your area should be away from family traffic.

- Discuss with family members your study goals and your need for a quiet place and private time to work. They may want to help you draw up a study schedule that will be satisfactory to everyone.

- Keep a study log. You can record what lesson was worked on, a list of topics studied, the time you put in, and the dates you sent your exercises to your instructor for grading.

- Work at your own pace, but move ahead steadily. The following tips should help you get the most value from your lessons.

  1. Look over the objectives carefully. They list what you are expected to know for the examination.

  2. Read the chapters carefully, and don't hesitate to mark your text—it will help you later. Mark passages that seem especially important and those that seem difficult, as you may want to reread these later.

3. Try to read an entire chapter at a time. Even though more than one chapter may be assigned in a lesson, you may find you can carefully read only one chapter in a sitting.

4. When you have finished reading the chapter, go back and check the highlights and any notes you have made. These will help you review for the examination.

Reviewing for the Final Exam

When you have completed the final exercise and practice test, you will have several items to use for your examination review. If you have highlighted important points in the textbook, you can review them. If you have made notes in the margins, check them to be sure you have answered any questions that arose when you read the material. Reread certain sections if necessary. Finally, you should go over your exercises.

The ProMgmt. Program

The National Restaurant Association Educational Foundation's ProMgmt. Program is designed to provide foodservice students and professionals with a solid foundation of practical knowledge and information. Each course focuses on a specific management area. For more information on the program, please contact the National Restaurant Association Educational Foundation at 800.765.2122 (312.715.1010 in Chicagoland) or visit our web site at **www.edfound.org**.

Lesson 1

INTRODUCTION TO FOOD AND BEVERAGE COST CONTROL

Student Objectives

After completing this lesson, you should be able to:

- Apply the basic formula used to determine profit.

- Express both expenses and profit as percentages of revenue.

- Compare actual operating results with budgeted operating results.

- Develop a procedure to record current sales.

- Compute percentage increases or decreases in sales over time.

- Develop a procedure to estimate future sales.

Reading Assignment

Read Chapters 1 and 2. Use this information to answer the questions and activities in Exercises 1 and 2.

Chapter 1 Exercise

1. Which of the following is/are required to earn a profit? Circle all that apply.

   a. Expenses in excess of revenue

   b. Planning

   c. Decision making

   d. Delegation

   e. Management

2. What are two ways that management can increase revenue in a foodservice establishment?

   • _____

   • _____

3. What are the four major foodservice expense categories?

   • _____   • _____

   • _____   • _____

4. Complete the following table.

%	Decimal	Fraction
20%	.20	1/5
58%		
	.33	
		3/4
65%		
		1/2
		60/200

5. Three hundred guests attended a party at Golden Acres Banquet Hall; 178 ordered chicken, and 122 ordered the prime rib. What percentage ordered the prime rib?

_____

6. Sales for the month of July at the Pelican Café were $6,250. Food and beverage expenses for the month totaled $2,580, labor totaled $1,985, and other expenses totaled $400.

   a. The manager hoped for a profit of $1,000. Did she reach her goal? _____
   b. What percentage of revenue went to expenses? _____
   c. What percentage of revenue was the manager's desired profit? _____

7. Below is a profit and loss statement for Josh's Hamburger Stop. Calculating dollar figures and percentages, use these figures to complete Josh's P&L statement.

Income	$450,000	100%
Expenses		
Food and beverage	190,000	_____
Labor	170,000	_____
Other	25,000	_____
Total expenses	_____	_____
Profit	_____	_____

8. Match each numbered term with its lettered definition.
   _____ (1) Budget
   _____ (2) Profit and loss statement
   _____ (3) Significant variation
   a. Variation in costs that management feels is a cause for concern
   b. Business's estimate of future revenue, expense, and profit
   c. Financial document showing an operation's expenses, revenue, and profit for a given period of time

9. Indicate whether each of the following is true (T) or false (F).

_____ a. The ultimate goal of any foodservice manager is to eliminate expenses.

_____ b. The formula Revenue − Expenses = Profit does not apply to nonprofit organizations.

_____ c. Inflation causes the purchasing power of a dollar today to be less than that of a dollar ten years ago.

_____ d. If you compute a cost percentage and get a number less than 1, you have probably made a mistake.

_____ e. On a profit and loss statement, expenses plus profit equal revenue.

_____ f. The 28-day approach to budgeting divides a year into 28 equal periods of 13 days each.

Chapter 2 Exercise

1. What is a sales history?

   _____

   _____

2. Vinnie's Pizza Place is located in a college town. This year, Vinnie introduced delivery service during football season and sales have increased. Below is a copy of Vinnie's sales records for the first two weeks of November.

Sales Period	Date	Cash Sales	Date	Cash Sales
Monday	Nov. 1	$301	Nov. 8	$406
Tuesday	Nov. 2	289	Nov. 9	380
Wednesday	Nov. 3	278	Nov. 10	372
Thursday	Nov. 4	325	Nov. 11	450
Friday	Nov. 5	370	Nov. 12	477
Saturday	Nov. 6	393	Nov. 13	444
Sunday	Nov. 7	425	Nov. 14	469

   a. Determine Vinnie's 14-day fixed average for the period given. _____

   b. Determine Vinnie's seven-day rolling average for each of the following periods.

   Nov. 1–7   _____

   Nov. 2–8   _____

   Nov. 3–9   _____

   Nov. 4–10   _____

   Nov. 5–11   _____

   Nov. 6–12   _____

   Nov. 7–13   _____

   Nov. 8–14   _____

   c. What is one advantage of using a rolling average to track sales figures?

   _____

3. Last year, Denny's Doughnut Shop served 10,747 customers.

   a. What was Denny's guest count for the year? _____

   b. Denny expects the number of customers served to increase by 6% this year. How many customers should he expect? _____

   c. If total sales last year were $37,558 for the doughnut shop, what was the check average? _____

   d. After making some menu additions, Denny expects the check average to increase by 9%. What is his forecasted check average? _____

   e. Project Denny's sales for this year. _____

4. Which of the following gives managers an indication of whether sales are improving, declining, or staying the same? Circle all that apply.

   a. POS systems

   b. Means

   c. Sales variances

   d. Check averages

5. Besides the sales history of an establishment, name three other factors that a food-service manager should consider when predicting future sales.

   • _____

   • _____

   • _____

Lesson 2

MANAGING THE COST OF FOOD AND BEVERAGES

Student Objectives

After completing this lesson, you should be able to:

- Use sales histories and standardized recipes to determine the amount of food products to buy in anticipation of forecasted sales.

- Purchase, receive, and store food products in a cost-effective manner.

- Compute the cost of food sold and food cost percentage.

- Use sales histories in conjunction with standardized drink recipes to develop a beverage purchase order.

- Compute the dollar values of bar transfers both to and from the kitchen.

- Compute an accurate cost of goods sold percentage for beer, wine, and spirits.

Reading Assignment

Read Chapters 3 and 4. Use this information to answer the questions and activities in Exercises 3 and 4.

Chapter 3 Exercise

1. Name five factors that might influence the number of guests you can expect to serve on a specific day.

   - _____
   - _____
   - _____

   - _____
   - _____

2. Which of the following arguments against using standardized recipes has any validity? Circle all that apply.

   a. They take too long to write up.

   b. My chef refuses to reveal his or her secrets.

   c. Many of my employees can't read English.

   d. They take too long to use.

   e. We tried them but lost some, so we stopped using them.

3. The standard recipe for rhubarb pie at Rebecca's Pie Shop calls for six cups of raw rhubarb and yields three pies. Rebecca wants to make eight pies. Using the factor method, how many cups of rhubarb will Rebecca need?

   _____

4. Match each food item on the left with its proper shelf life on the right.

   ____(1) Ground beef   a. 14 days

   ____(2) Flour   b. 6–12 month

   ____(3) Butter   c. 3 months

   ____(4) Cookies   d. 2–3 days

5. Indicate whether each of the following is true (T) or false (F).

_____a.   Edible portion (EP) refers to the weight or count of a product as delivered to the foodservice operator.

_____b.   To determine AP required, divide EP required by yield %.

_____c.   Suppliers tend to give better prices to high-volume operations.

_____d.   All orders should be placed using a purchase order form.

_____e.   Dry goods should be stored directly on the ground.

_____f.   Issuing begins the food production process.

6. What are the five questions to ask yourself when you are trying to figure out whether or not your course of action is ethical?

- _____
- _____
- _____
- _____
- _____

7. What is the difference between acceptance hours and refusal hours?

_____

_____

8. Every morning, the North Side Bakery sells approximately 350 doughnuts, muffins, and croissants to commuters waiting to take the local train to work. This means that every morning at 5:30 A.M., the manager must be at the bakery to receive the fresh products from the supplier. Should the manager use the FIFO or LIFO system to store them? Why?

_____

_____

9. Leslie works as a receiving clerk at an ice cream parlor. Every week, when the ice cream is delivered, Leslie steals a gallon for herself. The ice cream costs $11 a gallon, and the shop makes a 7% profit on every food dollar sold. How much money must the shop earn each week just to recover the cost of the stolen ice cream?

_____

10. Claire's Bistro had a beginning inventory of $8,165 for November. The meals that Claire provided her employees for the month totaled $533. Ending inventory was $3,344, food sales for the month were $31,468, and purchases totaled $4,299. What was Claire's food cost percentage for the month?

_____

Chapter 4 Exercise

1. Indicate whether each of the following is classified as a beverage-only establishment (B-O), beverage and food establishment (B-F), or beverage and entertainment/activity establishment (B-EA).

_____a.   Bowling alley

_____b.   Neighborhood bar

_____c.   Comedy club

_____d.   Hotel room service

_____e.   Banquet hall

_____f.   Winery

2. Indicate whether each of the following is true (T) or false (F).

_____a.   A state regulator who finds that a bar operator has violated the law can close a beverage operation down immediately.

_____b.   Keg beer is also known as ale.

_____c.   Forecasting the sale of house wines or any wine sold by the glass is similar to the process used to forecast beer sales.

_____d.   The shelf life of keg beer is the longest of all beer packaging types.

_____e.   Well liquors are those spirits that customers ask for by brand name.

_____f.   Beverage distributors do not sell products in less than one-case lots.

_____g.   Sales mix affects overall product cost percentage whenever guests are given a choice among several menu selections.

3. Which alcoholic beverage is the most perishable?

_____

4. Name four ways wine is sold.

• _____

• _____

• _____

• _____

5. Explain the two key system in the context of controlling access to beverage storage areas.

_____

_____

6. Abigail operates a family-style Italian restaurant. Last summer, she decided to add wine to her menu. In keeping with the preferences of her clientele, she bought several cases of mid- to low-priced wines and stored them under the bar between the refrigerator and a heating unit. By December, Abigail found that 25% of her wine had gone bad. What should she have done to prevent this?

_____

_____

7. Danny's Diner is a small bar and grill in a Midwestern city. Danny computed the following figures for the month of June:

Beginning inventory	$30,615
Beverage sales	$92,840
Transfers from bar	$765
Purchases	$12,355
Transfers to bar	$1,448
Ending inventory	$20,300

   a.   What is the cost of beverages sold for the month of June? _____

   b.   What is Danny's beverage cost percentage for the month? _____

8. What are the three ways to take liquor inventory?

- _____

- _____

- _____

Lesson 3

MANAGING THE PRODUCTION PROCESS AND PRICING

Student Objectives

After completing this lesson, you should be able to:

- Use management techniques to control the costs associated with preparing food and beverages for guests.

- Compute the actual cost of producing a menu item and compare that cost against the cost you should have achieved.

- Apply various methods to reduce cost of goods sold percentage.

- Choose and apply the best menu type to an operation you manage.

- Identify the variables you must consider before establishing your menu prices.

- Assign menu prices to menu items based on their cost, popularity, and ultimate popularity.

Reading Assignment

Read Chapters 5 and 6. Use this information to answer the questions and activities in Exercises 5 and 6.

Chapter 5 Exercise

1. Irene manages a fine-dining establishment. This week she is offering duck with plum sauce as a special item. Her daily sales forecast for the duck is 60 servings, and her margin of error is 7. Yesterday, the chef prepared 60 servings of duck and sold 45. How many new portions should be prepared today?

    _____

2. Name one product issuing principle that, if observed, can help management maintain product security.

    _____

3. Sean operates a corner bar in a small town. He operates a strict issues and requisition system, noting the total dollar value of all beverages issued for each day. Below are his records for the week beginning October 1.

Date	Issues	Sales
Oct. 1	$342	$458
Oct. 2	$402	$677
Oct. 3	$398	$427
Oct. 4	$379	$461
Oct. 5	$544	$668
Oct. 6	$439	$514
Oct. 7	$466	$505

    Based on the figures, what is Sean's beverage cost percentage estimate for the week?

    _____

4. Explain the difference between physical inventory and perpetual inventory.

    _____

    _____

5. Pierre is the chef at a large hotel restaurant in San Francisco. He prepares a special salmon recipe using only the freshest local fish. Pierre's production schedule tells him to prepare at least 80 portions of the salmon per day. His standardized recipe calls for 6 ounces of salmon fillets, 3 ounces of green beans, 1/3 cup of cream and 2 tablespoons of mixed herbs for each portion. Using the ABC inventory system, assign a category to each of the following items in Pierre's recipe.

____(1)   Salmon

____(2)   Capers

____(3)   Green beans

____(4)   Cream

____(5)   Herbs

6. When deciding whether or not to use a convenience item, what questions should a manager consider?

_____

_____

_____

7. What control issues are involved with each of the following?

   a.   Minibars

_____

   b.   Bottle sales

_____

   c.   Open bars

_____

8. Elisa is the newly hired manager of an upscale bar in the city. After being on the job for three weeks, she suspects that several of her bartenders have been stealing from the operation in a variety of ways. How might Elisa prevent the following types of theft that she believes are being committed?

a. Bartenders bringing in their own bottles, selling the products, and then pocketing the sales

   _____

b. Bartenders filling orders but not ringing them up

   _____

c. Bartenders watering down drinks

   _____

d. Bartenders substituting a less expensive well liquor for the call brand and then pocketing the price difference between the two items

   _____

9. How often should yield tests be conducted on meat items?

   _____

10. For the month of September, Monica budgeted her beverage cost percentage to be 28%. When she recomputed her actual product cost percentage, it turned out to be 5% higher that she had budgeted for. What are some ways she can reduce her cost?

   _____

   _____

Chapter 6 Exercise

1. Indicate whether each of the following is associated with a standard menu (S), a daily menu (D), or a cycle menu (C).

    ____a.   Allows management to respond quickly to changes in the price of the raw materials needed to produce the menu items

    ____b.   Recommended only for special situations because of the tremendous control drawbacks associated with its implementation

    ____c.   Typically used by traditional restaurants

    ____d.   Changes every day

    ____e.   Remains in effect for a specific time period

    ____f.   Gives guests a large number of menu items from which to choose

    ____g.   Does not utilize carry-overs effectively

    ____h.   Repeated on a regular basis

    ____i.   Utilizes carry-overs effectively

2. What is the difference between revenue and price?

    _____

    _____

3. A variety of factors influence menu prices. Which factor is being described in each of the following?

   a.   This factor is too closely monitored by the typical foodservice operator.

    _____

   b.   This factor is the most significant in overall pricing.

    _____

   c.   This factor is a function of both food quantity and how it is presented.

    _____

   d.   This factor may draw guests to a location the first time.

    _____

4. Julian decided to add homemade lemon sorbet to his dessert menu. He wants the product cost to be 16% of the menu price. If each serving of sorbet costs $0.55 to make, how much should Julian charge?

_____

5. Larry, the manager at Penny's Pasta, is assigning menu prices for two new items being offered at the restaurant. The cost of vegetarian lasagna is $5.15, and its food cost percentage is 43%. The cost of linguine with clam sauce is $7.37. Management's desired contribution margin for the linguine item is $6.00.

   a. How should Larry price the vegetarian lasagna?

   _____

   b. If the desired cost percentage for the lasagna was 39%, how would the lasagna be priced? Use a pricing factor to arrive at your answer.

   _____

   c. What price should Larry assign to the linguine with clam sauce menu item?

   _____

6. Indicate whether each of the following is true (T) or false (F).

   _____a. The key to keeping the selling price low in a salad bar or buffet situation is to apply the ABC inventory approach.

   _____b. When charging for beverages at a reception on a per person/per hour basis, management must have a good idea of how much the average attendee will consume during the length of the reception.

   _____c. Coupons have the effect of reducing sales revenue from each guest.

   _____d. Bundling refers to the practice of reducing all or most prices on the menu with the hope that total guest counts will increase to the point that total sales revenue also increases.

   _____e. Pricing wines by the bottle is controversial because of the small variance in cost among different vintages.

   _____f. Selecting specific menu items and pricing them as a group so that the single menu price is lower than if the items were purchased individually is known as value pricing.

7. Sally Ann, manager at Country Cookin', knows that the total product cost for her Sunday buffet is $305. If 144 guests are served, how much is the cost per guest?

_____

Lesson 4

CONTROLLING LABOR COST AND MANAGING OTHER EXPENSES

Student Objectives

After completing this lesson, you should be able to:

- Identify the factors that affect employee productivity.

- Develop appropriate labor standards and employee schedules for use in your foodservice operation.

- Analyze and evaluate your actual labor utilization.

- Assign other expenses in terms of being fixed, variable, or mixed.

- Differentiate controllable from noncontrollable other expenses.

- Compute other expense costs in terms of both cost per guest and percentage of sales.

Reading Assignment

Read Chapters 7 and 8. Use this information to answer the questions and activities in Exercises 7 and 8.

Chapter 7 Exercise

1. Match each numbered term with its lettered definition.

____(1) Labor expense

____(2) Job description

____(3) Separated

____(4) Minimum staff payroll

____(5) Productivity ratio

____(6) Payroll

____(7) Standard cost

____(8) Split shift

____(9) Cost of labor budget

____(10) Job specification

a. Gross pay received by employees in exchange for their work

b. Smallest number of employees required to operate a facility or department

c. Sum of all costs associated with maintaining a workforce

d. Output divided by input

e. Listing of the personal characteristics needed to perform the tasks of a particular job description

f. Listing of the tasks that must be accomplished by the employee hired to fill a particular position

g. Technique used to match individual employee work shifts with peaks and valleys of customer demand

h. Term used to describe employees who have either quit, been terminated, or in some other way have left the operation

i. Forecasted total sales 4 Labor cost % standard

j. Labor cost needed to meet established productivity standards

2. List three questions that would be inappropriate or illegal to ask during an interview with a young woman applying for the job of hostess of a foodservice operation. After each question, explain why it should not be asked.

- _____
  _____

- _____
  _____

- _____
  _____

3. Explain why employee training is essential to managing payroll costs.

   _____
   _____

4. Mandy operates a neighborhood hamburger restaurant in a large metropolitan area. She has 30 employees. In the past year, Mandy has hired 14 new employees as replacements.

   a. What is Mandy's turnover rate?

   _____

   b. From the information given, can you determine involuntary employee turnover rate and voluntary employee turnover rate? Why or why not?

   _____

5. Jamaal has the following information from his records for the week of February 1 to February 7:

Cost of labor $5,600

Total labor hours   889

Sales $14,646

Number of guests served   621

    a. Determine the following measures of productivity:

        (1) Labor cost percentage _____

        (2) Sales per labor hour _____

        (3) Labor dollars per guest served _____

        (4) Guests served per labor hour _____

    b. List one advantage and one disadvantage to using each of the productivity measures named in part a.

        (1) _____

          • _____

        (2) _____

          • _____

        (3) _____

          • _____

        (4) _____

          • _____

6. Jose plans to open a pizza operation that is part of a nationwide chain. He knows that the first step in controlling labor costs is to determine standards of productivity. Unfortunately, Jose has never managed a restaurant of this type and therefore has no sales or labor figures on which he can base his standards. What other information might he use?

_____

7. Which of the following is/are true with respect to scheduling employees? Circle all that apply.

    a. The cost of labor budget can be calculated by dividing forecasted total sales by labor cost % standard.

    b. Employees should be scheduled only when they are needed.

    c. If labor is purchased on a daily basis, labor costs should be monitored on a daily basis.

    d. In an on-call system, employees who are off-duty are required to check in with management on a daily basis to see if volume is such that they may be needed.

8. Loretta budgeted $8,460 for labor in November. Actual labor costs were $9,321. What percentage of the labor budget was actually spent in November?

_____

9. Three professionals were frustrated that they had to wait for their "express" lunches for nearly 25 minutes. When they complained to their server, he offered them dessert on the house for their inconvenience.

    a. What is the term used to describe the "power" that the server used to appease and satisfy his customers?

_____

    b. How does this power increase employee productivity?

_____

Chapter 8 Exercise

1. Indicate whether each of the following other expenses is:

   a. fixed (F) or variable (V)

   b. controllable (C) or noncontrollable (N)

	a	b
(1) Take-home containers	_____	_____
(2) Insurance	_____	_____
(3) Franchise fees	_____	_____
(4) Billboard rental	_____	_____
(5) Real estate taxes	_____	_____
(6) Advertising	_____	_____
(7) Paper napkins	_____	_____
(8) Parking lot rental	_____	_____

2. In examining the expenses incurred by her Italian restaurant over the past year, Maxine is classifying her costs as fixed or variable. She pays $4,000 plus 2% of the operation's total sales revenue per month for rent. How should Maxine classify this cost?

   _____

3. Claire manages a take-out pizza stand. Her variable expenses consist primarily of paper products, such as pizza boxes, paper cups, lids, napkins, and paper bags. Claire keeps tight control over her inventory and does not suspect her employees of theft. She just finished calculating her variable expenses for the month of May and found that they increased by 4% over the previous month.

   a. Claire assumes that the increase is a sign that business is improving. Do you agree? Why or why not?

   _____

   b. What should Claire do to determine whether or not her assumption is correct?

   _____

4. As the newly hired manager of Bagels and Beyond, Hank has established one of his primary management goals: to reduce total variable cost expenses. Is this an appropriate goal? Why or why not?

_____

_____

5. When a cost is within an acceptable variation range, Jeremy does not intervene. He acts only when a fixed expense is too high or a variable expense is out of control. What kind of management does Jeremy employ?

_____

6. Donna knows that the sum total of her other expenses for the month of June was $4,890.

   a. Determine her other expense cost percentage if total sales for June were $76,540.

_____

   b. Determine her other expense cost per guest if 20,500 guests were served.

_____

7. How does employee turnover affect other expenses related to labor?

_____

_____

Lesson 5

ANALYZING RESULTS AND MONITORING PERFORMANCE

Student Objectives

After completing this lesson, you should be able to:

- Prepare an income (profit and loss) statement.

- Analyze sales and expenses using the P&L statement.

- Evaluate your facility's profitability using the P&L statement.

- Analyze a menu for profitability.

- Prepare a cost/volume/profit analysis.

- Establish a budget and monitor performance to the budget.

Reading Assignment

Read Chapters 9 and 10. Use this information to answer the questions and activities in Exercises 9 and 10.

Chapter 9

1. Explain why each of the following interest groups needs financial information about a foodservice establishment.

   a. The government

   _____

   b. New suppliers

   _____

   c. Partners and investors

   _____

2. Explain the difference between the following sets of terms.

   a. Record keeping and managerial accounting

   _____

   _____

   b. Average inventory and inventory turnover

   _____

   _____

3. What is the purpose of the Uniform System of Accounts for Restaurants?

   _____

   _____

4. Mauricio is the owner and operator of a fajita bar in Myrtle Beach, South Carolina. Below is the income statement for Mauricio's first two years of business.

	Last Year	%	This Year	%
Sales				
Food	$1,723,044	____	$2,074,288	____
Beverages	415,668	____	438,992	____
Total sales	_____	____	_____	____
Cost of Sales				
Food	697,770	____	755,005	____
Beverages	90,814	____	93,881	____
Total cost of sales	_____	____	_____	____
Gross Profit				
Food	_____	____	_____	____
Beverages	_____	____	_____	____
Total gross profit	_____	____	_____	____
Operating Expenses				
Salaries and wages	601,995	____	660,500	____
Employee benefits	90,014	____	99,687	____
Direct operating expense	112,458	____	122,660	____
Utility services	68,440	____	80,455	____
Occupancy	115,000	____	115,000	____
Total operating expenses	_____	____	_____	____
Operating Income	_____	____	_____	____
Interest	81,445	____	79,455	
Income before income taxes	_____	____	_____	____
Income taxes	59,808	____	70,033	____
Net income	_____	____	_____	____

a. Complete Mauricio's income statement.

b. Compute Mauricio's overall increase in sales from last year to this year.

_____

c. List three reasons why Mauricio might have experienced total sales volume increases in the current year.

- _____

- _____

- _____

d. Is Mauricio's income statement an accurate reflection of the restaurant's financial health? Why or why not?

_____

_____

Chapter 10

1. Marissa manages a small Mexican restaurant in a major metropolitan area. She is considering making some menu changes. Below is a copy of her menu with each item's cost and selling price.

<u>Beef fajita</u>

Cost:	$1.35
Number sold:	5,000
Selling price:	$4.25

<u>Cheese enchilada</u>

Cost:	$1.05
Number sold:	6,000
Selling price:	$2.75

<u>Chicken burrito</u>

Cost:	$1.15
Number sold:	8,000
Selling price:	$3.50

<u>Bean and cheese burrito</u>

Cost:	$0.92
Number sold:	3,500
Selling price:	$2.50

a. What is the total cost percentage for all four menu items together?

_____

b. What is the average selling price?

_____

c. Analyze Marissa's menu using the food cost percentage matrix.

_____

_____

d. Explain appropriate strategies that Marissa might employ in marketing each of these menu items.

_____

_____

_____

_____

2. Kurt, the manager at Fresh Fish and More, is analyzing his menu using the contribution margin approach.

   a. What is his goal, based on the matrix method that he has selected to analyze his menu?

   _____

   b. What is the contribution margin per menu item?

   _____

   c. Which two variables will Kurt use for the analysis?

   _____

   d. Why might Kurt decide not to use the contribution margin approach—or any other matrix method for that matter?

   _____

3. Assuming that Marissa's variable costs account for 30% of her total sales, use the information in Question 1 to help Marissa conduct a goal value analysis.

   a. Compute the goal value of Marissa's total menu.

   _____

   b. Compute the goal values for each of Marissa's menu items and rank them in order of highest to lowest goal value.

	Goal value	Rank
Beef fajita	_____	_____
Cheese enchilada	_____	_____
Chicken burrito	_____	_____
Bean and cheese burrito	_____	_____

   c. Which item(s) fall below the overall goal value score?

   _____

   _____

   d. Should Marissa replace this/these item(s)? Why or why not?

   _____

   _____

4. Sammy's Sizzlin' BarBQ has fixed costs of $50,000, with a contribution margin percentage of 55% and a contribution margin per unit (guest) of $8.00.

    a. What is Sammy's break-even point in sales?   _____

    b. What is his break-even point in guests served?   _____

5. David wants to prepare a budget for the coming year.

    a. Sandra, the operator of the establishment, thinks that preparing a budget is an unnecessary waste of time. What arguments can David use to convince her of the importance of making a budget?

_____

_____

    b. What type of budget does David want to create?

_____

6. Why do some operators use the yardstick method of calculating expense standards?

_____

_____

Lesson 6

Student Objectives

After completing this lesson, you should be able to:

- Identify internal and external threats to revenue dollars.

- Create effective countermeasures to combat internal and external theft.

- Establish and monitor a complete and effective revenue security system.

- Identify areas where technology can be used to improve the cost control system.

- Evaluate cost control technology enhancements based on their ability to improve existing control programs.

- Monitor technological developments within the cost control area.

Reading Assignment

Read Chapters 11 and 12. Use this information to answer the questions and activities in Exercises 11 and 12.

Chapter 11 Exercise

1. What is the most efficient way for managers to verify revenue security?

   _____

2. Don oversees the management of twenty family pizza restaurants located in various cities in the Midwest. Over the past year, he has observed each operation and suspects that there is a variety of guest theft. What steps should his employees take to prevent the kinds of fraud that Don suspects is taking place?

   a. Guests walking the bill

   _____

   b. Guests using invalid credit cards

   _____

   c. Guests engaging in the quick-change routine

   _____

3. Why should managers insist that manual guest checks be filled out in pen?

   _____

4. Nina manages a cafeteria that serves employees and guests in a large hospital. At the end of the day, she notices that the guest checks, cash register sales figure, and cash drawer all balance. However, total revenue relative to the amount of food product used is short. Nina also notices that an unusually large number of voids has occurred during the day. She suspects her cashier of theft.

   a. What can she do to prevent this from happening in the future?

   _____

   b. If Nina had proof that the cashier had stolen money and the cashier had been bonded, could the foodservice operation be reimbursed for the stolen money?

   _____

5. What are the four key points that foodservice managers should consider when developing a revenue security system?

- _____

- _____

- _____

- _____

6. Indicate whether each of the following is true (T) or false (F).

_____a.   Guest checks refer to actual revenue received by the cashier in payment for products served.

_____b.   Both the cashier and a supervisor should verify sales receipts.

_____c.   No product should be issued from the kitchen or bar unless a permanent record of issue is made.

_____d.   A guest check control form is used to track the checks issued to service personnel.

7. What are the four basic payment arrangements used in the typical foodservice operation?

- _____

- _____

- _____

- _____

8. Name a practice used to help prevent embezzlement in a foodservice establishment.

_____

Chapter 12 Exercise

1. Explain the difference between software and hardware.

   _____

   _____

2. Name five ways that computer software programs can help foodservice managers and their employees in the area of food and beverage production.

   • _____

   • _____

   • _____

   • _____

   • _____

3. Match each of the following hardware-related terms on the left with its definition on the right.

   ____(1) Monitor

   ____(2) Hand-held device

   ____(3) Microprocessor

   ____(4) Modem

   ____(5) Hard drive

   ____(6) Printer

   ____(7) RAM memory

   a. Powers the computer's central processing unit

   b. Responsible for processing speed

   c. Provides permanent storage for software programs and data files

   d. Palm-size bar code reader

   e. Provides the ability to connect to the Internet

   f. Used to create a record of charges for guests, as well as in-house marketing materials

   g. Should be 17-inches or larger

4. Which of the following is considered a communication device? Circle all that apply.

   a. Word processing program

   b. Multimedia

   c. E-mail

   d. Pager

   e. Internet

5. Indicate whether each of the following is true (T) or false (F).

_____a.   If the cost of a tool exceeds its value to your operation, its purchase is questionable.

_____b.   Technology items need routine maintenance and can break down.

_____c.   The fastest service response time to service problems is 24 hours.

_____d.   There are several rating systems in place for hospitality-related technology items.

_____e.   The closer the location of a vendor to an operational unit, the more successful the managers at that unit will be in establishing a sold relationship with the vendor.

6. Name three sources of information related to advances in cost control technology.

- _____

- _____

- _____

Study Outline

Chapter 1

1. Professional foodservice managers handle all of the functions of product sales.
2. In both commercial and noncommercial operations, **revenue minus expenses equals profit.**
   a. Businesses incur expenses. These expenses must be managed in such a way that an operation achieves its desired profit levels.
   b. All foodservice operations need revenue in excess of expenses to thrive.
   c. Careful planning is required to earn a profit.
3. **Revenue** dollars are the result of units sold. To increase revenue, a manager can:
   a. increase the number of guests served.
   b. increase the amount that each guest spends.
4. In the foodservice industry, expenses are typically divided into **food costs, beverage costs, labor costs,** and **other costs.**
   a. Other costs usually include the costs of utilities, rent, linen, and other tools needed to operate a business.
5. **Percent** refers to a portion of 100 or of the total. Thus, 10 percent, or 10%, means 10 out of 100 and can also be expressed as 10/100 (fraction form) or as 0.10 (decimal form).
   a. Expense divided by revenue equals expense %.
   b. Desired profit divided by revenue equals desired profit %.
6. The basic financial operating statement of a foodservice operation is the **profit and loss** or **income statement.**
   a. The profit and loss statement shows the income, expenses, and profit of an operation over a period of time.
   b. Total revenue is given a value of 100%, and all other values—various costs and profit—are expressed as percentage portions of total income.

7. Another crucial financial operating document, the **budget,** allows managers to plan income, expenses, and sales volume for a period and to compare planned and actual figures.

   a. Budgets are used to help managers buy goods and beverages, plan marketing and promotional campaigns, and hire employees.

   b. The percentage of the budget actually used is referred to as **performance to budget.**

   c. The **28-day period approach** divides a year into 13 equal periods of 28 days each.

   d. The formula Actual 4 Budget 5 % of budget compares actual expense to the amount budgeted.

Chapter 2

1. When managers predict the number of guests to be served and the revenues to be generated in a given future time period, they have created a **sales forecast.**

2. A **sales history** is the systematic recording of all sales during a predetermined period of time.

   a. **Sales to date** is the cumulative total of sales reported.

3. An **average** is the value arrived at by adding the quantities in a series and then dividing the sum by the number of items.

   a A **fixed average** is determined for a specific time period.

   b. A **rolling average** is the average amount of sales or volume over a changing period of time.

   c. A **weighted average** weights the number of guests with how much they spend in a given time period.

4. The number of people served is known as the **guest count.**

5. The **check average** or **average sales per guest** is computed by dividing total sales by the number of guests served.

6. **Sales variance** are changes from previously experienced sales levels. Sales this year minus sales last year equals sales variance.

   a. Effective managers also calculate **percentage variance**—the percentage change in sales from one period to the next.

7. Revenue forecasts can be determined by multiplying sales last year by the percentage increase estimate and then adding sales last year.

8. The guest count forecast is determined by multiplying guest count last year by the percentage increase estimate and then adding the guest count last year.

Chapter 3

1. The **popularity index** is the percentage of total guests choosing a given menu item from a list of choices.
   a. Popularity index = Total number of a specific menu item sold 4 Total number of all menu items sold.
   b. The popularity index helps managers make good decisions about the quantity of each item that should be prepared.
2. **Standardized recipes** are the cornerstone of any serious effort to produce consistent, high-quality food products at an established cost.
3. To adjust recipes for quantity, a foodservice manager can use the factor method or the percentage technique.
   a. Using the **factor method,** a manager computes a conversion factor by dividing yield desired by current yield and then multiplying each ingredient in the recipe by the conversion factor to arrive at the proper amount of that ingredient.
   b. The **percentage method** involves computing the percentage of each ingredient in relation to the total weight needed.
4. Inventory levels are determined by storage capacity, item perishability, vendor delivery schedule, potential savings from increased purchase size, operating calendar, relative importance of stock outages, and value of inventory dollars to the operator.
5. A **purchase point** is the point when an item should be reordered. It is typically designated by the **as need method** or the **par level method.**
6. Operators use **production specifications** to let vendors know exactly the characteristics they need in inventory items.
   a. Specifications include product name, packaging desired, pricing unit, standard or grade, weight range/size, processing and/or packaging, container size, intended use, and any other information that helps describe what is desired.
7. **Product yield** tells managers how much **edible portion** (EP) is available from **as purchased** (AP) food.
   a. The formulas for finding EP and AP quantities use a **waste percentage** found by Product loss 4 AP weight = Waste %.
   b. Then the following formulas are used:
      EP required 4 Yield percentage = AP required.
      AP required 3 Yield percentage = EP required.

8. **Bid sheets** are often used by managers to compare price quotes from several vendors in order to make well-informed buying decisions.

9. **Ethics** is defined as the choices of proper conduct made by an individual in his or her relationships with others.

10. A **daily inventory sheet** includes items in storage areas, units of purchase, and par values preprinted on the sheet.

11. Once a vendor is chosen and specifications are used to communicate exact product characteristics, the operator submits a **purchase order** to the vendor listing the items to be delivered, the agreed-upon prices, and the anticipated delivery date.

12. All deliveries should be checked and weighed carefully and then compared to both the purchase order and the vendor's invoice to be sure the operation is paying for what it received.

    a. Proper receiving includes appropriate location of storage area, proper tools and equipment provided to receiving personnel, accurate delivery schedules, and proper training.

13. Food items must be stored correctly to help control their costs.

    a. A system of product use, most commonly the **first-in, first-out (FIFO)** method, helps ensure that food is not wasted because of spoilage.

    b. Proper storage temperatures are essential to prevent food spoilage.

14. To determine the **cost of food sold** for a period, a manager or employee must keep either a physical or perpetual inventory of all items in storage. The following formula is used: Beginning inventory for a period 1 Purchases 2 Ending inventory 2 Employee meals 5 Cost of food sold.

    a. The cost of food sold is used to find the operation's **food cost percentage:** Cost of food sold 4 Food sales = Food cost percentage.

    b. **Daily cost of food sold** can be found using a six column form and the following formulas: Purchases today 4 Sales today = Cost percentage today, and Purchases to date 4 Sales to date = Cost percentage to date.

Chapter 4

1. The three types of operations that serve alcoholic beverages can be grouped as beverage-only, beverage and food, and beverage and entertainment/activity.

2. **Alcoholic beverages** can be classified as either beer, wine, or spirits.

3. Training employees to serve alcoholic beverages properly is essential.
    a. **Dramshop laws** shift the liability for acts committed by an intoxicated patron to the server or operation that supplied the intoxicating beverage.
4. Forecasting guest item selection is a difficult process for beverage sales because there is a large number of possible items from which patrons can choose.
    a. Beer sales are forecasted by tracking what percentage of guests select beer and what kind of beer they select.
    b. Wine sales are forecasted both by the bottle and by the glass.
    c. Spirit sales are forecasted by estimating the sales for every mixed drink and determining the amount of each spirit ingredient that will be needed.
5. Standardized recipes and standard portion sizes are developed for mixed drinks in the same way they are for food.
    a. Beverage cost percentage can be found with the formula: Cost of beverages consumed 4 Beverage sales = Beverage cost percentage.
6. When purchasing beverage products, several levels of quality are usually selected.
    a. Beer operators typically carry three to ten types of beer.
    b. Operators must determine if they will sell wine by the glass, split or half bottle, carafe, or bottle.
    c. Managers must determine which **well brands** (those that are used when guests don't ask for a specific brand of liquor) and **call brands** (those guests ask for by brand name) to carry.
7. Beverages must be stored properly to manage and control their costs.
    a. Spirits should be kept in dry storage at temperatures between 70°F and 80°F (21°C and 27°C).
    b. Beer in kegs must be stored at refrigerated temperatures of 36°F to 38°F (2°C to 3°C).
    c. Canned and bottled beer should be kept in dry storage between 50°F and 70°F (10°C and 21°C).
    d. Wines should be stored at temperatures between 50°F and 65°C (10°C and 18°C). Wine must also be protected from direct light and moisture.

8. Operators must also manage the cost of items associated with the preparation and service of beverage products.

   a. Transfers from the bar should be subtracted from ending inventory for a period.

   b. Transfers to the bar should be added to ending inventory.

9. The three commonly-used methods for valuing opened containers of alcoholic beverages are weight, count, and measure.

10. The **sales mix** is the series of guest purchasing decisions that result in a specific food or beverage cost percentage.

    a. Guests will ultimately determine the overall cost percentage through sales mix.

Chapter 5

1. **Production schedules** are used to plan the amount of each menu item that will be prepared daily.

   a. To determine how much of each menu item to prepare, managers use the formula: Prior day's carry-over 1 Today's production 5 Today's sales forecast 1/2 Margin of error.

2. Food and beverage inventory items are controlled through a systematic issuing system.

   a. All employees should fill out a requisition form for the items they need from the storage area.

   b. A common way to measure beverages is the **empty for full system,** in which employees must return empty bottles before receiving new full ones.

   c. Having servers identify a guest check number when requesting wine will ensure that wine issues will match wine sales at the end of each shift.

   d. Careful beverage issuing helps management estimate daily costs.

3. The following formulas help managers control the issuing of beverages.

   a. Issues today 4 Sales today 5 Beverage cost estimate today.

   b. Issues to date 4 Sales to date 5 Beverage cost estimate to date.

4. Items in inventory are controlled through a **physical inventory** of each item on hand or a **perpetual inventory,** in which items are tracked through written or computerized records.

   a. **Bin cards** are used to record a beverage inventory product's additions to and deletions from inventory.

   b. The ABC inventory system helps managers determine which items deserve special attention, as well as those that require less time managing.

5. **Category food cost percentage** is a food cost percentage computed on a portion of total food usage, by using the cost of food/sales formula.

   a. Proportion of total product costs can be calculated by dividing cost in each product category by total cost in all categories.

6. Managing the food production process requires control of waste, overcooking, overserving, carry-over utilization, and the make-or-buy decision.

7. Various beverage control systems can be used, depending on the amount of control an operator thinks is appropriate.

   a. Free pour should never be allowed in the preparation of the majority of drinks by bartenders.

   b. **Jiggers,** metered bottles, and beverage "guns" can be used to dispense a predetermined portion of product.

   c. Total bar systems combine sales information with product dispensing data to create a complete revenue and product management system.

8. Different areas of a beverage operation must be controlled in different ways.

   a. Minibars can be controlled by housekeeping staff replenishing missing bottles and then reporting what has been used.

   b. Bottle sales are controlled by tracking full and empty bottles.

   c. Managers of **open bars** must have especially tight control of portion sales.

   d. Banquet operations use a form of bottle sales control.

9. Careful employee training and monitoring by supervisors are essential to ensure that products are not stolen by employees.

   a. Managers must constantly be on the lookout for bar theft, which most often occurs when bartenders fill orders but do not ring them up, bring in extra product, over- and underpour, make incorrect change, dilute the product, steal the product, or substitute less expensive products for more expensive ones.

10. **A standardized recipe cost sheet** records the ingredient costs required to produce the items sold by an operation.

11. To determine actual recipe costs, it is sometimes necessary to conduct a **yield test** to arrive at actual EP ingredient costs. To arrive at a figure for product yield percentage, the following formulas are used:

 a. Product loss 4 AP weight 5 Net waste percentage.

 b. 1.00 (Total) 2 Net waste percentage 5 Product yield percentage.

 c. EP weight 4 AP weight 5 Product yield percentage.

12. **Attainable food cost** is the cost of goods sold figure that should be achievable given the product sales mix of a particular operation.

 a. To determine an establishment's operational efficiency ratio, divide actual product cost by attainable product cost.

13. To reduce product cost percentages, managers can decrease portion size relative to price, vary recipe composition, adjust product quality, achieve a more favorable sales mix, ensure that all product purchased is sold, and increase prices relative to portion size.

Chapter 6

1. There are three types of foodservice menus.

 a. A **standard menu** is the one most often seen in full-service operations of all types and decors.

 b. A **daily menu** changes every day.

 c. A **cycle menu** is used for a set amount of time and then is repeated.

2. Minor menu changes can be incorporated on a regular basis by offering daily or weekly **menu specials.**

3. Managers must develop a positive **price/value relationship,** ensuring that menu items match prices that guests are willing to pay and for which they feel a good value is received.

4. The following formulas are used in developing menu pricing:

 a. Revenue 2 Expense 5 Profit.

 b. Price 3 Number sold 5 Total revenues.

5. Factors influencing menu price include local competition, service levels, guest type, product quality, portion size, ambience, meal period, location, and sales mix.

6. To determine price with the product cost percentage method, the following formula is used: Cost of a specific food item sold 4 Food cost percentage of that item 5 Food sales (selling price) of that item.
   a. Alternatively, a cost factor can be assigned to each desired food cost percentage: Pricing factor 5 1.00 4 Desired product cost %.
   b. Then use this formula: Pricing factor 3 Product cost = Menu price.
7. A menu item's **contribution margin** is found through the use of one of the following formulas: Selling price 2 Product cost 5 Contribution margin or Product cost 1 Contribution margin desired 5 Selling price.
8. Pricing decisions that call for unique approaches involve the use of coupons, value pricing, bundling, salad bars and buffets, bottled wine, and beverages at receptions.

Chapter 7

1. **Labor expense** includes salaries and wages, as well as other expenses related to employees, such as FICA and unemployment taxes, worker's compensation, insurance, pension/retirement plan payments, employee meals, training expenses, transportation, uniforms, housing, vacation/sick leave, employee incentives, and bonuses.
2. **Payroll** is the gross pay each employee receives in exchange for his or her work.
   a. Employee payroll is usually divided into **fixed** or **variable labor,** depending on whether employees' hours and wages change with level of sales and business volume.
3. Managers assess employees' productivity with the formula: Output 4 Input 5 Productivity ratio.
4. The employee selection process begins with written **job descriptions** for every position and **job specifications** that describe the personal characteristics needed to perform the tasks in a particular job description.
   a. When employers actually begin to select employees for vacancies, they usually use applications, interviews, testing, and/or background checks.
5. Effective employee training must be carefully planned to ensure that the right employees are being trained using the most appropriate methods.
6. Effective employee supervision means supplying employees with what they need to do the best job they can, including providing them with proper equipment and rewards for doing a good job.

7. Scheduling should be based on estimates of business volume and productivity ratios.

8. Short, frequent breaks increase employee productivity and morale, and may be mandated by law.

9. Effective managers provide an environment that makes it easy for employees to be motivated.

10. An efficiently-designed menu combined with simplified preparation methods enables kitchen employees to be more productive.

11. When deciding to make or buy menu items, managers must consider product quality and product cost.

12. Managers must provide employees with the tools and equipment necessary to effectively do their jobs.

13. The following formulas are used by managers to measure the efficiency of employees and to control labor costs:

    a. Cost of labor 4 Total sales 5 Labor cost percentage.

    b. Total sales 4 Labor hours used 5 Sales per labor hour.

    c. Cost of labor 4 Guests served 5 Labor dollars per guest served.

    d. Guests served 4 Cost of labor 5 Guests served per labor dollar.

    e. Guests served 4 Labor hours used 5 Guests served per labor hour.

14. A six-column productivity report is used to record daily cost of labor and cost of labor to date, daily sales and sales to date, and daily labor cost percentage and labor cost percentage to date.

15. The payroll cost management process requires four steps.

    a. Determine productivity standard.

    b. Forecast sales volumes.

    c. Schedule employees using productivity standards and forecasted sales volume.

    d. Analyze results.

16. Empowering employees to make decisions that affect their jobs results in positive, loyal workers and allows managers to do higher-level, management-related tasks.

Chapter 8

1. **Other expenses** are not classified as food, beverages, or labor, but they are directly related to them. They include the following:

   a. Direct operating expenses

   b. Music and entertainment

   c. Marketing

   d. Utility services

   e. General and administrative expenses

   f. Employee benefits

   g. Repairs and maintenance

   h. Rent

   i. Interest

   j. Depreciation

2. Other expenses can be further divided into **fixed, variable,** or **mixed costs,** as well as into **controllable** or **noncontrollable costs.** All of these expenses should be monitored and managed through efficient employee and management practices.

3. The following formulas help managers measure and control their other expenses.

   a. Other expense 4 Total sales 5 Other expense cost percentage.

   b. Other expense 4 Number of guests served 5 Other expense cost per guest.

4. Managers can lower other expenses by reducing the following:

   a. Costs related to food and beverage operations

   b. Costs related to labor

   c. Cost related to facility management

   d. **Occupancy costs**

Chapter 9

1. The basic form of business analysis used by foodservice managers and operators is **cost accounting,** in which the costs of doing business are examined, and budgets are prepared and maintained.

2. To help them maintain organized books and operating statements, most foodservice operators follow the National Restaurant Association's **Uniform System of Accounts for Restaurants.** It is designed to achieve uniformity among various operations in the industry.

3. The income statement is the key management tool for cost control.

    a. Income statements list revenue first, then expense, and finally the difference between revenue and expense.

    b. The USAR is divided into three sections: gross profit, operating expenses, and nonoperating expenses.

4. To compute overall sales increases or decreases, managers should go through the following steps:

    a. Determine sales for this accounting period.

    b. Calculate this period's sales minus last period's sales.

    c. Divide the difference by last period's sales to determine percentage variance.

5. **Inventory turnover** refers to the number of times the total value of inventory has been purchased and replaced in an accounting period. The following formulas are used to determine inventory turnover:

    a. Beginning inventory value 1 Ending inventory value 5 Average inventory value.

    b. Cost of food consumed 4 Average inventory value 5 Food inventory turnover.

6. To analyze beverage and labor expenses, managers use the following formulas:

    a. Cost of beverages consumed 4 Average beverage inventory value 5 Beverage inventory turnover.

    b. Salaries and wages expense 4 Total sales 5 Salaries and wages expense percentage.

7. Profit margin, also known as **return on sales (ROS),** is computed as Net income 4 Total sales.

    a. Gains or losses in net income can be measured by profit variance: (Net income this period 2 Net income last period) 4 Net income last period 5 Profit variance percentage.

Chapter 10

1. Menu analysis tells managers how successful menu items are individually and how well the menu is doing overall.

    a. **Matrix analysis** allows menu items to be placed into categories based on whether they are above or below menu item averages.

    b. In the **food cost percentage method,** the food cost percentage for each item is measured and compared to the desired food cost percentage.

    c. An item's **popularity** is its percentage of the total items sold.

    d. An item's **contribution margin** is its selling price minus its cost.

e. **Goal value analysis** evaluates each menu item's food cost percentage, contribution margin, and popularity, and includes the analysis of each item's nonfood variable costs and its selling price.

2. In **cost/volume/profit analysis,** managers can determine at what level of sales an operation will recover its costs, as well as the level of sales needed to generate a specific profit level.

   a. When sales volume equals the sum of variable and fixed costs, an operation has reached its **break-even point.**

   b. To calculate the break-even point, managers should use one of the following formulas:

   Fixed costs 4 Contribution margin 5 Break-even point in sales.

   Fixed costs 4 Contribution margin per unit (guest) 5 Break-even point in guests served.

3. **Minimum sales point** (MSP) is the dollar sales volume required to justify staying open for a given period of time.

   a. To calculate the MSP, a manager needs to know the **minimum operating cost,** which can be found by computing Food cost percentage + Variable cost percentage.

   b. Then one of the following formulas should be used:

   Minimum labor cost 4 (1 2 Minimum operating cost) 5 MSP.

   Minimum labor cost 4 (1 2 Food cost percentage + Variable cost percentage) 5 MSP.

4. A budget is a financial plan that details the operational direction of a foodservice establishment, as well as its expected financial results.

   a. Managers prepare long-range budgets for periods of three to five years, annual budgets, and short-range achievement budgets.

   b. Budgets must be continually analyzed, maintained, updated, and revised.

Chapter 11

1. A revenue security system ensures that Product issues 5 Guest charges 5 Sales receipts 5 Sales deposits.

2. External threats to revenue security can take the following forms:

   a. **Walking** or **skipping the bill:** Managers and employees should carefully track where customers are in their meals, present the check promptly after the meal is served, and take payment in a timely manner.

b. **Fraudulent payment:** Managers and employees should check the validity of personal checks before accepting them for payment. All credit card transactions should be verified with the credit card company, and procedures required by each card issue should be carefully followed.

   c. The **quick-change artist** tries to confuse the cashier into giving him or her too much change. Cashiers must be trained well and instructed to notify management immediately if there is any suspicion of attempted fraud through quick-change routines.

3. The best way to prevent theft by servers is to manage a closely-monitored guest check system that ensures that the value of products sold and the amount of revenue received equal each other.

   a. Written **guest checks** should be required for each sale.

   b. Many operators use a **pre-check/post-check system** for guest checks.

   c. Servers should be required to use pens when filling out guest checks, or managers can provide them with guest checks made from nonerasable paper.

   d. Many operators use a computerized system to record sales, tally check totals, and compare money collected with money that should have been collected.

4. When a cashier is responsible for the collection of money, several areas of potential fraud exist.

5. Employees of a foodservice establishment can be **bonded** as a way to insure against employee theft.

6. An effective revenue security system will help managers verify product issues, guest charges, sales receipts, and sales deposits.

Chapter 12

1. Foodservice revenue and expense management will be heavily influenced by the expanding capabilities of technology in the future.

2. Operators seeking to use technology are interested in new information, more accurate information collection, more convenient collection of information, better communication of information, and/or improved analysis of information.

3. **Software** consists of the actual computer programs that generate the cost-related information that foodservice managers and employees will use in their jobs.

4. **Hardware** consists of the point of sales system terminals, personal computers, time clocks, inventory/bar code–reading equipment, and other devices required to manage the cost control software purchased.

5. **Communication devices** often used by foodservice managers include cellular telephones, fax machines, e-mail, pagers, and the Internet.

6. Before selecting and purchasing any technological enhancement to a foodservice establishment's existing cost control efforts, managers should consider cost, complexity of the technology, the system's warranty, maintenance issues, upgradability, and reliability of both the products and the vendors.

7. To stay up-to-date with the commercial application of technological advances, managers can attend trade shows, join professional associations, read industry publications, contact current and competitive vendors, take technology related classes, and, if the facility is part of a national chain or large company, contact the parent organization.

Practice Test

This practice test contains 80 multiple-choice questions that are similar in content and format to those found on the Educational Foundation's final examination for this course. Mark the best answer to each question by circling the appropriate letter. Answers to this practice test are on page 73 of this Student Workbook.

Lesson 1: Introduction to Food and Beverage Cost Control

1. In May, the Pizza Palace spent $42,116 and earned $101,773. What was the operation's monthly profit?
   A. $58,861
   B. $59,657
   C. $60,330
   D. $62,465

2. If an operation forecasts earnings of $500,000, and its desired profit is $50,000, its ideal expense is
   A. $400,000.
   B. $450,000.
   C. $550,000.
   D. $740,000.

3. In most cases, which costs are greatest for a foodservice establishment?
   A. Food costs
   B. Beverage costs
   C. Labor costs
   D. Other costs

4. How is 300% expressed as a decimal?
   A. 0.003
   B. 0.03
   C. 0.30
   D. 3.00

5. Cajun Delight's profit is $358,000, and its income is $957,000. What is the operation's profit percentage?
   A. 26.7%
   B. 37.4%
   C. 43.8%
   D. 51.0%

6. An operation's profit percentage is 17.8%. This means that for each dollar of sales, it earns how much profit?
   A. $0.0178
   B. $0.1780
   C. $1.78
   D. $17.80

7. A forecast of projected revenue, expense, and profit is called a
   A. P&L statement.
   B. 28-day period.
   C. budget.
   D. performance report.

8. For an existing foodservice operation, the first place a manager should look when predicting future sales volume is
   A. the operation's sales histories.
   B. industry journals and periodicals.
   C. general sales figures for the area.
   D. national economic indicators.

9. An operation's manager determines the average sales for every Thursday in each month. What type of average is the manager calculating?

   A. Mean
   B. Rolling
   C. Total
   D. Fixed

10. An operation earns $6,400 daily from an average of 555 guests. What is the operation's check average?

   A. $8.67
   B. $11.53
   C. $12.01
   D. $12.50

11. Glen's Steak House earned $450,400 in sales last year, and management estimates that it will earn $507,150 in the coming year. By what percentage does management predict that sales will increase?

   A. 11.7%
   B. 12.6%
   C. 14.8%
   D. 16.0%

12. Most POS systems are designed to give managers information regarding

   A. the number of guests served.
   B. the operation's rolling average.
   C. food and beverage inventory.
   D. employee scheduling.

13. A weighted average weights the number of guests with

   A. the number of waitstaff available for a shift.
   B. the specific types of items that they order.
   C. how much they spend in a given time period.
   D. the total sales figure for a given time period.

14. This year's sales for The Fish Fry were $828,400, and last year's sales totaled $801,416. The variance is

   A. $26,984.
   B. $54,817.
   C. $100,889.
   D. $1,629,816.

Lesson 2: Managing the Cost of Food and Beverages

15. A manager has determined that 175 portions of prime rib should be prepared out of a total of 650 menu entrees. What is the popularity index for prime rib?

   A. 19.6%
   B. 26.9%
   C. 37.1%
   D. 47.5%

16. An operation's recipe for 12 portions of Chicken Cordon Bleu calls for 3 cups of bread crumbs. Using the factor method, how many cups of bread crumbs will be needed to yield 20 portions?
    A. 4
    B. 5
    C. 6
    D. 7

17. The amount of time a food item retains its maximum freshness, flavor, and quality while in storage is called its
    A. safety stock.
    B. purchase point.
    C. shelf life.
    D. par level.

18. The Vegetarian Garden has purchased and trimmed 40 pounds of cauliflower and ended up with 22 pounds of trimmings for stock. What is the waste percentage for this cauliflower?
    A. 25%
    B. 35%
    C. 45%
    D. 55%

19. A foodservice operation that gets bids from many vendors and then buys only those items that each vendor has on sale or for the lowest price is known by suppliers as a(n)
    A. opportunity cost.
    B. cherry picker.
    C. auditor.
    D. slacker.

20. Which of the following questions should foodservice managers ask themselves to help them decide if a specific action is ethical?
    A. Does it hurt anyone?
    B. Can I get it for a lower price?
    C. Will anyone find out?
    D. Will it cost me my job?

21. Which term is used to indicate that an ordered item has not been delivered as promised?
    A. Credit
    B. Shorting
    C. Padding
    D. FIFO

22. A vendor's invoice lists 5 cases of tomatoes at $17.20 per case, 5 cases of lettuce at $20.15 per case, and 4 cases of carrots at $18.00 per case. What is the invoice's total?
    A. $156.60
    B. $205.00
    C. $258.75
    D. $285.75

23. State dramshop laws hold food-and-beverage operators and employees liable for
    A. injuries and deaths to third parties caused by intoxicated patrons.
    B. liquor sales to minors or habitual alcoholics.
    C. not paying appropriate taxes on commercially-sold liquor.
    D. injuries to intoxicated patrons.

24. Which of the following types of sales is the most difficult to track?

   A. Beer sales
   B. Wine sales
   C. Spirit sales
   D. Vintner sales

25. A one-liter bottle of liquor contains how many ounces?

   A. 24.0
   B. 27.9
   C. 30.3
   D. 33.8

26. Spirits poured when the guest does not specify a particular brand name when ordering are called

   A. tapped brands.
   B. well brands.
   C. call brands.
   D. premium liquors.

27. In a two key system, one key is in the possession of the individual responsible for the beverage area and the other key is kept

   A. hanging on a wall near the beverage area.
   B. in a sealed envelope in a safe or in another secured area of the operation.
   C. by the security director.
   D. in a broken case.

28. Ricardo's ending inventory for March was $67,446. Transfers to the bar totaled $245, and transfers from the bar were $1,640. What was the cost of beverages sold for the month?

   A. $66,051
   B. $66,511
   C. $68,841
   D. $69,331

Lesson 3: Managing the Production Process and Pricing

29. The manager of Chicken Lovers has set tomorrow's sales forecast for Chicken Marsala at 65. The carryover from the previous day is 7, and the manager has added a margin of error of 5. How many portions of Chicken Marsala should the production staff prepare?

   A. 53
   B. 63
   C. 67
   D. 77

30. Which of the following forms is used when employees need supplies from inventory?

   A. Purchase order
   B. Purchase specification
   C. Requisition
   D. Production forecast

31. An actual count and valuation of all inventory on hand, taken at the close of each accounting period, is called a(n)

   A. perpetual inventory.
   B. physical inventory.
   C. issued inventory.
   D. standardized inventory.

32. In the ABC inventory system, the items in category C are those that

   A. have the lowest value.
   B. require routine control and record keeping.
   C. are stored in refrigeration.
   D. are classified as convenience products.

33. Which of the following should never be allowed in the preparation of the majority of drinks served by bartenders?

   A. Jigger
   B. Beverage gun
   C. Free pour
   D. Total bar system

34. The total product loss for 12 pounds of turkey is 4 pounds 10 ounces. What is the net product yield percentage?

   A. .385
   B. .487
   C. .551
   D. .615

35. If the actual food cost for The Pasta Inn was $1,420 for the week and the attainable food cost was $1,295, what was the restaurant's operational efficiency ratio?

   A. 88.1%
   B. 90.3%
   C. 103.3%
   D. 109.7%

36. Which type of menu tends to dominate those segments of the foodservice business where the guest selects the location of the dining experience?

   A. Daily menu
   B. Standard menu
   C. Cycle menu
   D. Special item menu

37. One advantage of employing a standard menu is that

   A. personnel can be trained to produce a wide variety of foods.
   B. management can respond quickly to changes in the price of raw materials needed to produce the menu items.
   C. the ordering process is simplified.
   D. daily creations are viewed with great anticipation.

38. The term revenue means the amount

   A. charged to one guest.
   B. spent by all guests.
   C. earned by waitstaff personnel as gratuities.
   D. paid as dividends to shareholders.

39. Which of the following is the most significant factor in overall pricing?
    A. Portion size
    B. Sales mix
    C. Competitors' prices
    D. Inflation

40. Fettuccine Alfredo has a selling price of $12.95 and a food cost percentage of 42%. What is the item's food cost?
    A. $3.24
    B. $5.44
    C. $7.51
    D. $7.92

41. A menu item costs $3.64, and management desires a contribution margin of $5.00. What is the most appropriate selling price for the item?
    A. $8.95
    B. $9.95
    C. $10.95
    D. $11.95

42. A restaurant has catered a private wedding party with an open bar for guests. After the party, a total of $1,830 worth of liquor and beverages has been served to 258 guests. What is the product cost per guest?
    A. $5.06
    B. $6.49
    C. $7.09
    D. $9.15

Lesson 4: Controlling Labor Costs and Managing Other Expenses

43. Which of the following is most likely to be a fixed-cost employee?
    A. Purchasing agent
    B. Host or hostess
    C. Buser
    D. Grill cook

44. It is most likely that foodservice employees will work hardest for a manager who
    A. makes decisions and then tells employees about them.
    B. gives employees feedback only during yearly performance evaluations.
    C. shares a vision of the organization with employees.
    D. trains only those employees who frequently make mistakes.

45. Which of the following labor costs is considered controllable by management?
    A. Payroll
    B. Employment taxes
    C. Insurance premiums
    D. Pension plan payments

46. Which of the following questions does the Equal Employment Opportunity Commission suggest that an employer consider when deciding to include a particular question on an employment application or in a job interview?
    A. Is there a better way to ask this question?
    B. Does this question focus on an applicant's qualifications for the job?
    C. Does this question tend to screen out minorities or females?
    D. Will the answer to this question be too vague?

47. If each server at Miller's Café can serve an average of 80 guests in a night, how many servers will be needed if 640 guests are expected?
    A. 6
    B. 8
    C. 10
    D. 12

48. In the past year, 21 employees at Griller's Pub have quit and 6 have been terminated. If there were 50 employees in the workforce, what is Griller's turnover rate?
    A. 14.8%
    B. 36.4%
    C. 49.2%
    D. 54.0%

49. Which of the following is a drawback to using the sales per labor hour figure when measuring productivity in the hospitality industry?
    A. It can hide daily or weekly highs and lows.
    B. It varies with changes in the price of labor.
    C. It ignores price per hour paid for labor.
    D. It is time consuming to compute.

50. Chop Suey Express used 472.5 labor hours last week and served 689 guests. How many guests did the operation serve per labor hour?
    A. 1.46
    B. 2.34
    C. 5.68
    D. 6.86

51. What is the first step in the payroll cost management process?
    A. Forecast sales volume.
    B. Determine productivity standards.
    C. Schedule employees.
    D. Establish company objectives.

52. Working with food manufacturers and wholesalers to reduce product packaging waste is known as
    A. management by exception.
    B. source reduction.
    C. liquidation.
    D. comping.

53. Which of the following is considered a direct operating expense?

    A. Advertising
    B. Water
    C. Exterminating
    D. Technology used for entertainment

54. A flat lease amount of $4,800 per month plus 1.5% of total sales revenue is an example of a(n)

    A. fixed expense.
    B. variable expense.
    C. mixed expense.
    D. annual expense.

55. Which of the following might be done to reduce other expense costs related to labor?

    A. Use a competitive bid process.
    B. Provide excellent training.
    C. Include split shifts when scheduling employees.
    D. Create job-share programs.

Lesson 5: Analyzing Results and Monitoring Performance

56. What is the primary purpose of the Uniform System of Accounts?

    A. Ensures that financial information is presented in a useful and consistent way
    B. Imposes a mandated methodology for tracking financial information
    C. Allows for the combination of balance sheets and income statements
    D. Identifies net income generated after all appropriate expenses of a business have been paid

57. Which of the following is the key management tool for cost control?

    A. FICA
    B. Income statement
    C. Performance report
    D. COLA

58. The three sections of the Uniform System of Accounts for Restaurants are arranged

    A. by type of expense (fixed, variable, mixed).
    B. according to the unique needs of each foodservice operation.
    C. from most controllable to least controllable by the foodservice manager.
    D. chronologically.

59. The details associated with the sales, expenses, and profits on an aggregate statement can be found in

A. the operation's files.
B. supporting schedules.
C. POS systems.
D. returns on sales.

60. Landlubbers had sales of $274,382 this period and $257,183 last period. What is the operation's percentage variance?

A. −6.3%
B. +6.3%
C. −6.7%
D. +6.7%

61. Jerry's Steakhouse had a beginning inventory in March totaling $39,812 and ended the month with $36,900. Purchases for March totaled $12,875. What was Jerry's average inventory value?

A. $26,344
B. $38,356
C. $49,775
D. $52,687

62. Sophie's net income for this year was $215,202, while total sales were $2,640,699. What was Sophie's profit margin for the year?

A. 8.1%
B. 9.2%
C. 10.0%
D. 10.7%

63. Which of the menu analysis methods is the oldest and most traditional?

A. Food cost percentage
B. Contribution margin
C. Goal value
D. Cost/volume/profit analysis

64. Paul's Fishery sold 800 entrees in an accounting period from among eight possible menu choices. If Paul uses the food cost percentage method in his analysis of his menu, an item will be considered high in popularity if it sold how many times during the period?

A. 10
B. 80
C. 100
D. 180

65. If a menu item has high popularity but also a high food cost percentage, which marketing strategy might be used?

A. Decrease the price of the item.
B. Increase the portion size.
C. Take the item off the regular menu and run it as a special.
D. Reduce the prominence of the item on the menu.

66. One drawback to the matrix method is that it
    A. is extremely time consuming and complex.
    B. replaces menu averaging techniques with algebraic formulas.
    C. forces some items to be below average.
    D. requires the use of sophisticated computer software programs.

67. In the goal value formula, C stands for which of the following?
    A. 1.00 − Food cost %
    B. Selling price
    C. 1.00 − (Variable cost % + Food cost %)
    D. Item popularity

68. Total sales for Molly's Waffle House were $180,000 for the accounting period. If the contribution margin was $95,000 for the period, what were Molly's total costs for the period?
    A. $52,000
    B. $85,000
    C. $180,000
    D. $275,000

Lesson 6: Protecting and Improving a Cost Control System

69. When a guest consumes a product but leaves the foodservice operation without paying the bill, that customer has been said to have done which of the following?
    A. Slipped the scene
    B. Hit and run
    C. Walked the bill
    D. Committed embezzlement

70. Most commonly, guests fraudulently pay foodservice operations by
    A. passing counterfeit money.
    B. writing bad checks.
    C. using invalid credit or debit cards.
    D. presenting false credit records.

71. To prevent service personnel from giving the proper guest check to the guest, collecting payment and then destroying the guest check but keeping the money, many operators
    A. administer an honesty test to people applying for the job of server.
    B. implement a pre-check/post-check system for guest checks.
    C. use only those guest checks made from nonerasable paper.
    D. insist that service personnel total guest checks with an adding machine or calculator.

72. Purchasing an insurance policy against the possibility that an employee will steal is called
    A. bonding.
    B. verification.
    C. shorting.
    D. leverage.

73. No product should be issued from the kitchen or bar unless
    A. the guest signs the check.
    B. the server has paid for it.
    C. a guest control form is used.
    D. a permanent record of issue is made.

74. Which of the following is true about a payment arrangement in which the guest pays the server and the server pays the cashier?
    A. Customers can more easily skip their checks.
    B. Guests must stand in line to pay their bills.
    C. Guests may have to wait longer than they want to in order to settle their bill.
    D. The arrangement is used primarily in quick-service establishments.

75. Which of the following is a communication device?
    A. Spreadsheet program
    B. Laptop computer
    C. Modem
    D. Hand-held bar code reader

76. In which area can foodservice managers most effectively use the technological tools that are available today?
    A. Managing the cost of food products
    B. Managing the food and beverage production process
    C. Managing food and beverage pricing
    D. Managing the cost of labor

77. Interfacing various software programs means doing what to them?
    A. Debugging them
    B. Connecting them
    C. Upgrading them
    D. Installing them

78. As a general rule, what size monitor should a foodservice establishment buy?
    A. 15-inch
    B. 17-inch
    C. The largest screen that fits the establishment's application
    D. The largest screen that the establishment can afford

79. Many standard warranties on technology products specify which of the following?
    A. Upgrade requirements
    B. 24-hour response time to service problems
    C. Locations of service centers
    D. Expiration dates

80. Which of the following is most likely
a reliable source for information
about advances in cost control
technology?

A. Guests
B. Servers
C. Stockholders
D. Competitive vendors

Practice Test Answers and Text Page References

1.	B ....p. 4	28.	A...............p. 165	55.	B ....p. 357
2.	B ....p. 5	29.	B ....pp. 178–79	56.	A...............p. 367
3.	A.................p. 7	30.	C...............p. 179	57.	B ....p. 368
4.	D ....pp. 9–11	31.	B ....p. 192	58.	C...............p. 369
5.	B ....p. 13	32.	A...............p. 194	59.	B ....p. 371–72
6.	B ....p. 13	33.	C...............p. 206	60.	D ....p. 374
7.	C.................p. 18	34.	D ....p. 219	61.	B ....p. 379
8.	A.........pp. 27–28	35.	D ....p. 220	62.	A.........p. 387–88
9.	D ....pp. 32–33	36.	B ....p. 238	63.	A...............p. 396
10.	B ....p. 36	37.	C...............p. 238	64.	C...............p. 396
11.	B ....p. 44	38.	B ....p. 244	65.	D ....p. 400
12.	A.................p. 28	39.	B ....p. 249	66.	C...............p. 403
13.	C.................p. 37	40.	B ....p. 250	67.	B ....p. 406
14.	A.................p. 39	41.	A...............p. 251	68.	B ....p. 414
15.	B ....p. 55	42.	C...............p. 261	69.	C...............p. 443
16.	B ....p. 61	43.	A...............p. 277	70.	C...............p. 444
17.	C.................p. 64	44.	C.........p. 278–79	71.	B ....p. 449
18.	C.................p. 77	45.	A...............p. 278	72.	A...............p. 452
19.	B ....p. 83	46.	C...............p. 283	73.	D ....p. 454
20.	A.................p. 85	47.	B ....p. 291	74.	C...............p. 461
21.	B ....p. 97	48.	D ....p. 296	75.	C.........p. 484–85
22.	C.................p. 102	49.	C...............p. 303	76.	A...............p. 486
23.	A.......pp. 138–39	50.	A...............p. 306	77.	B ....p. 481
24.	C.......pp. 142–43	51.	B ....p. 318	78.	C...............p. 483
25.	D ....p. 155	52.	B ....p. 340	79.	B ....p. 487
26.	B ....p. 155	53.	C...............p. 342	80.	D ....p. 489
27.	B ....p. 160	54.	C.........p. 346–48		